IVIES

RONALD WHITEHOUSE

D0493587

HarperCollins*Publishers*

Products mentioned in this book

Benlate* + 'Activex' 2	contains	benomyl
'Nimrod'-T	contains	bupirimate/triforine†
'Rapid'	contains	pirimicarb
'Sybol'	contains	pirimiphos-methyl

*Benlate is a registered trade mark of Du Pont's
†Triforine is a product of Celamerck

Read the label before you buy; use insecticides safely

Editors Diana Brinton, Joey Chapter
Designer Joyce Mason
Picture research Moira McIlroy
Production Craig Chubb

First published in 1991 by
Harper Collins Publishers
London

**A CIP catalogue record for this book
is available from the British Library.**

ISBN 0-00-412601-7

Photoset by Litho Link Ltd, Welshpool, Powys, Wales
Printed and bound in Hong Kong by Dai Nippon Printing Company

Front cover: Hedera helix 'Pedata' by John Glover
Back cover: Ivy enhancing a stone statue by Tania Midgley

CONTENTS

INTRODUCTION

Ivy is such a well-known plant that it forms an unnoticed background in the countryside and garden. Yet the versatility of ivy for covering ground, climbing walls, trailing from baskets and tumbling from containers, in a very wide choice of varieties in colour and leaf shape, makes it one of the least-exploited evergreen garden plants.

Ivy is an ancient plant native to Europe, Asia and North Africa, but imported into the Americas. It was so readily at hand that it was used as a decorative and celebratory symbol 3,000 years ago by the Egyptians, and later by the Romans. In our own mediaeval times a 'bush' of ivy on a stake was used as the sign for a tavern. The 'alestakes' often extended so far across the highway that riders struck their heads against them, until in 1375 an Act of Parliament restricted their length to seven feet.

Ivy's popularity reached a peak in Victorian times, when it was used extensively inside the home as well as in the garden. Now, with the introduction of many new and exciting varieties, it is once again enjoying favour.

A garden plant Ivy is unlike any other plant or shrub in its growth. Although it is very easy to grow and is trouble free, it is important that you understand the nature of the plant if you are to get the best from this lovely evergreen.

Ivy has two distinct growing forms, a habit known as dimorphic. The first form is juvenile and the second is adult. The juvenile form is the one almost always used in gardens, and this is the form shown in most of the photographs. The adult form, which is called arborescence, comes naturally when the ivy has finished all the climbing it wishes to do and feels the need to flower and produce seed. This change of growth usually takes place when the ivy reaches good light, either at the top of a wall or high in a tree.

Ivies used for ground cover sometimes do this after a few years, even at ground level.

The flowering stems grow leaves of a different shape to those lower on the same stem. Irrespective of the leaf shape of the juvenile form, the new leaves become oval and form bracts to the flowering heads.

RIGHT At the arborescent stage, ivy produces delicate flowers in order to propagate itself.

BELOW LEFT Any garden can be enhanced with ivies. Here, *Hedera colchica* 'Dentata Variegata' covers a plain brick wall.

Erect ivies Although ivies for garden planting are in their juvenile form, it is possible to find 'tree ivies'. These are ivies propagated from the adult form, and they start life directly as free-standing shrubs which will flower and fruit, even when small plants.

There is also a small group of ivies known as 'erect ivies'. These grow upright as specimen shrubs without help, and will not climb or trail. There is also one ivy called 'Conglomerata' which is exclusively a prostrate form and is therefore only able to creep along the ground.

The species The generic or botanical name of ivy is *Hedera*. Botanists have not yet decided on the number of species in the genus. Seven species are cultivated widely, of which the most important is *helix*, or English ivy, and this has by far the largest number of cultivars.

The seven species are as follows:

azorica, obviously from the Azores; *canariensis*, not so obviously from North Africa (botanists want to rename this *algeriensis*); *colchica*, the Persian ivy; *helix*, the British common ivy; *nepalensis*, from Nepal; *pastuchovii*, the Russian ivy, and *rhombea*, from Japan.

The first three species have two cultivars, each of which are particularly useful in gardens. There are more than 300 varieties of the British common ivy, *Hedera helix*.

The different leaf shapes of ivy, from bird's foot to fan, and all the variegations, from splashed yellow to spotted cream or speckled white, are sports or mutations. What this means to the gardener is that all these have to be propagated vegetatively, by taking cuttings, by layering, or even by grafting. The species, which of course are green, may be grown from seed, but if you sow a seed from a variegated sort you will produce a green ivy.

GROWING IVIES

Ivy is a woodland plant. If you keep this in mind, success in growing it is assured. Partial shade or dappled sunshine with a leafmould mulch is home from home to an ivy plant. For the gardener, this gives endless scope, because walls and fences that are north, east and west facing all fill this bill, as do ground-cover beds in the shadow of these walls. Even south-facing walls need not be excluded, provided the correct species and variety of ivy is selected.

LEFT Graceful cascades of ivy cover a stone urn and are trained along steps, softening the division between two levels of this garden.

OPPOSITE A young ivy starting its climb.

BELOW RIGHT Site your plants in groups of three at least 30cm (1ft) from a fence.

A leafmould mulch might not be readily available, but as good, and easier to obtain, are 'Forest Bark' Ground and Composted Bark or Chipped Bark, which make ideal mulches.

Ivies are not fussy as to soil type. It used to be said that they preferred chalk or lime, but recent tests have shown no marked difference in growth between ivies planted in clay, sand or chalk. What does make a difference is access to nutrients.

The same basic rules apply whether you are growing ivies as climbers, as trailers or as ground cover. For best results, the site should be deeply forked to break the pan that may be at the base of the top soil. Ivies are deep rooted, and any difficulties that the roots have in establishing themselves will be reflected in reduced growth.

Organic material, well incorporated into the soil, is an obvious help, but failing this bonemeal or a similar, slow-acting material is a good alternative. Do not be tempted to add chemical fertilizers at this stage – the needs of ivies are low, and surplus nutrients may scorch the roots. Remove weeds as you dig, and leave the whole area well turned over and friable.

Avoid simply digging a planting hole and filling it with good quality compost. This new and loose material will either dry out in a drought period or collect water in a rainy one. Either way, this will adversely affect the plant.

Climbers For planting, you will need a trowel, a knife, and a quantity of short lengths of galvanized wire. These should be about 10cm (4in) long and bent in the shape of hairpins. Finally, you will require a bucket of 'Forest Bark' Ground and Composted Bark.

Ivies do not suffer from competition in the way that other shrubs do; indeed, they are aggressive competitors in their own right. The stems root in the soil as they trail across the ground, taking up nutrients from many points rather than from a single root. This fact can be used to obtain quick coverage, as it is possible to plant three ivies at each station instead of a single specimen.

To cover a wall or fence, the general rule is to plant well away from it and allow the trails of ivy to run towards the wall, rooting in the freshly-turned soil as they go. How far away you plant depends on the structure, but you must avoid the permanently dry area near the wall and use the space that receives rain. To cover a normal timber garden fence, for example, your planting

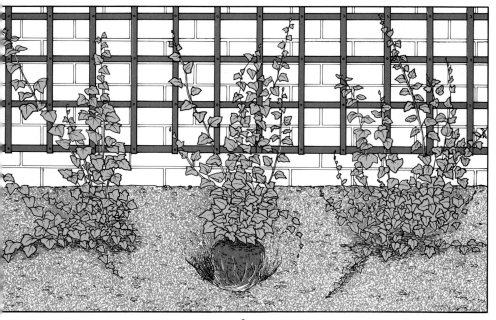

LEFT Pin down trails with bent wire to help them root.

FAR RIGHT Ivies are ideal for containers provided they are not allowed to dry out.

BELOW RIGHT *Hedera colchica* 'Dentata Variegata' used for ground cover in a mixed border.

hole should be trowelled 30cm (1ft) away. For ivy grown against a brick or stone wall, 60cm (2ft) should be allowed. Against a house wall with overhanging eaves, 90cm (3ft) is not too much.

Planting young climbers Assuming that you have young ivies in pots, soak these first by standing them in a bowl of water.

At the chosen site, trowel out a hole rather larger all round than the pot. If you are planting ivies in groups of three, the individual holes should be 30cm (1ft) apart, with 90cm (3ft) between each group. Single ivies should be planted 90cm (3ft) apart.

Take your soaked ivy plant. If it is on a cane, cut the ties with your knife and remove the cane. Knock the plant from its pot, then place it in the hole in such a way that the trails fall naturally towards the wall. If they don't, turn the plant until this is the case. Push and firm the soil that surrounds the plant. Always plant a little deeper than the existing pot depth; if the ivy plant is

short of leaves at its base, you can plant it as much as 5cm (2in) deeper.

Now take the bucket of 'Forest Bark' Ground and Composted Bark; lift the ivy trails with one hand, and with the other spread a good thick layer of mulch.

The trails now running towards the wall should be pinned down with the bent wire clips. Soon, the trails will root from each leaf joint and new growth will make its own way up the wall.

Planting for ground cover Prepare the ground and plant ivies for ground cover in exactly the same way as for climbing ivies. Make sure that you remove all perennial weeds from the soil, or these will give endless problems in the future. Ivies will eventually cover the ground so well that they will inhibit annual weeds, but just a short stolon of couch grass or bindweed will multiply and spoil your bed. Large-leaved ivies may be planted at centres spaced 90cm (3ft) apart, and smaller-leaved sorts closer, some 60cm (2ft) apart.

After the ivies have been planted, annual weeds may be controlled with simazine. Use a watering-can with a fine rose, and simply sprinkle the solution, made up according to the packet instructions, on to the soil around the ivies. This is a very simple method of control, and will not harm the ivies.

Finally, a layer of mulch will help to retain moisture while the young plants are establishing themselves.

Planting in containers The secret of success with ivies in containers of all kinds is never to allow the compost to dry out.

Conversely, ivies do not like to be waterlogged. The ideal container should therefore offer good drainage, which will allow a considerable degree of overwatering, and it should be filled with a compost mix that will retain moisture yet drain surplus water freely.

For pots, baskets and containers with a capacity of up to 2l (3½pt), you can do no better than to use John Innes potting compost No. 3. This is a coarse, loam-based mixture which will help to get the ivies off to a good start.

For larger containers, it is worth taking the time to make your own coarser mix from the simple formula of one-third sterilized loam, one-third chopped bark and one-third coarse grit. The grit can be of any stones that are less than 5mm (¼in) in diameter. Mix with this a compost-based fertilizer.

This mixture will be too heavy for use in large hanging baskets, and the formula for these should therefore be modified by using perlite instead of the coarse grit.

PLANTING FOR A PURPOSE

Ivies can fill many design needs in a garden, from climbing upwards to cover a vertical surface, to tumbling downwards to soften a hard edge, or growing prostrate in a shady corner.

Climbers Most ivies are natural climbers. They cling to rough surfaces by means of roots that grow on the opposite side of each leaf node.

The trails progress from their tips, feeling their way and climbing as they go. Their natural climbing surface is bark or stone, and it is helpful to keep in mind that existing growth will not cling. Only new growth will take root, so if you feel tempted to buy a tall ivy plant, do not think that you can prop this against a wall as an instant self-clinging climber.

You can, of course, obtain an immediate effect in this way, but the existing growth will only blow around in the wind, and its tips will have a hard job to get a grip on the wall. In the long run a smaller plant will make a better climber.

Some species and varieties cling better than others, and you can use this knowledge to suit your needs.

ABOVE A number of different ivies transform a pergola into a leafy haven.

BELOW *Hedera helix* 'Buttercup' helps a stone trough blend in with its surroundings.

For example, if you want a self-clinging ivy that will need no support, and you have a sound wall or fence, then choose an *azorica* or *canariensis* or any of the 'vining' *helix* varieties.

If you have an old wall to cover, and this may not be too sound in construction, you will be looking for a climber that clings lightly, in which case you could choose any *colchica*. The varieties of this species do not cling so tightly and therefore need some support.

The varieties of *helix* fall into two groups. One group is the 'vining' ivies; the other is 'self-branching' sorts. The former should be used for climbing; the latter are suitable for trailing, containers and ground cover. These ivies are identified in the descriptions at the end of the book.

You do not need to have a wall or fence to enjoy using ivies as climbers. Ivies can make dramatic and spectacular garden features on posts, on tree stumps, on a pergola or even woven into a chain-link fence. Their advantage, of course, is that they are evergreen, so their colour is there for you to see and enjoy in winter, when most other climbers are dormant.

Associations You may choose to grow other climbers in association with ivies and get the best of both worlds. Ivies make an attractive climbing combination with clematis, both the species, with their lovely seedheads, and the large-flowered hybrids. Climbing roses and honeysuckle also make good companions for ivies.

The possible associations of ground-cover ivies should also be considered; these can look very effective when underplanted with spring bulbs of all kinds, for example.

BELOW Striking use of *Hedera helix* 'Marginata Major' with a conifer.

BOTTOM *Hedera colchica* 'Dentata', in its arborescent form, surrounds a tree.

13

Ground cover All *helix* self-branching varieties make good ground cover. You might choose a green ivy with a leaf shape that catches your eye – and there are some quite unusual ones – or a variegated ivy, to give you either gold (yellow) or silver (white) colour.

Variegated ivies do best in a sunny situation, whereas green will be better in a shady spot. Some *helix* cultivars look so fancy and delicate that there is a mistaken belief that they are tender. In fact, all are normally hardy in Britain.

Variegated leaves may become weather-beaten by frosts and storms, but these leaves are soon replaced when warmer weather comes along.

Perhaps the best variegated silver *helix* ivy for ground cover is 'Glacier'. Two good cream forms are 'Eva' and 'Anne Marie'. A gold form that has been much improved in recent years is 'Goldchild'.

When you come to green ivies, the choice is almost too numerous. For very hardy cover in exposed places, 'Hibernica' is undoubtedly safe but rather unadventurous; try 'Trustee' as a bold yet tough alternative.

For normal purposes, an excellent green – in fact, a deep bronze – cultivar is 'Ivalace', with its crinkled, glossy leaves which catch the sunlight. Another attractive curly ivy, and one that is ideal for covering ground, is the lighter-green 'Manda's Crested'.

OPPOSITE Variegated ivies make a perfect foil for marguerites and pansies in a window-box.

LEFT For extensive ground cover, perhaps in a border which requires minimum maintenance, ivies are both attractive and extremely effective.

For spectacular large-leaved ground cover, the *colchica* varieties may be used. Both 'Dentata Variegata' and 'Sulphur Heart' are very successful used in this way.

Planters and hanging baskets Ivies lend themselves to container gardening, and their flowing trails have the advantage of all-year-round appeal. Consequently, they can replace summer-flowering plants in winter, and fully utilize containers and baskets that would otherwise be redundant.

Many varieties of *helix* are suitable and prove very hardy in exposed hanging baskets. An excellent green cultivar is 'Irish Lace', which has small, finely-fingered leaves. A recommended silver-variegated small-leafed ivy is 'Jubi-lee'. Another attractive silver ivy is 'Little Diamond', and a golden-variegated form is 'Ceridwen'.

Larger-leafed ivies do well in tubs and urns. Again, *helix* varieties are best, and the spear-shaped 'Bro-kamp' trails well. Another rich-green curly-leaved sort is 'Boskoop', which also throws numerous trails.

Variegated ivies that are worth considering for tubs and urns include 'Kolibri', 'Adam' and 'Sagit-tifolia Variegata'.

For special purposes A number of ivies lend themselves to special situations. There is one true minia-ture in the *helix* range, called 'Spetchley', which has extremely tiny deep-green leaves that never grow larger than 1cm (⅜in). This is very useful for planting in spaces in dry walls, between paving slabs and in similar places. It is also an excellent ivy for a bottle garden.

There are several ivies that have small leaves, but are not true miniatures, and these will also do well in such situations. A particularly bushy silver-variegated form is 'Ardingly'; a good golden ivy is 'Aurea Variegated', and a green variety to try is 'Arran'.

There is one prostrate ivy with crinkled leaves, appropriately named 'Conglomerata'. This most unusual ivy is well worth planting in a rock garden.

For specimen planting, try something completely different in the form of an upright ivy, sometimes called 'the candelabra ivy'. You might, for example, choose 'Erecta', which has broad leaves, closely spaced on upright stems, or try 'Congesta', which has leaves with narrower points. These cultivars require no support.

ABOVE The smaller-leaved ivies are suited to hanging baskets, where their delicate trails are an impressive feature.

LEFT An upright, or 'candelabra', ivy makes an unusual specimen plant for a bed or patio.

A 'tree ivy', or 'arborescent', makes an interesting single specimen. This is the adult form of ivy and is propagated directly from flowering stems, so that even tiny plants will flower in their first year of growth. This is ideal for gardeners who wish to encourage late insects, butterflies and bees, since it is autumn flowering.

Houseplant ivies You might be of the belief that ivies in the home would have to be distinct varieties, but this is not so. Suppliers and growers of houseplant ivies select ordinary but attractive cultivars, almost always *helix* varieties, and grow them in warm glasshouse conditions.

This produces a lush and brightly-coloured ivy which both looks and is tender. Consequently, you may bring into your conservatory, greenhouse or home any variety of ivy that takes your fancy. On the other hand, you may take a houseplant ivy and, when it is thoroughly hardened off, use it in the garden.

Take advantage of this knowledge to fill your home with young ivy plants, which you can propagate from garden cuttings.

ABOVE Tree ivies are a delightful sight in a garden, and provide additional interest in the autumn with their flowers.

LEFT Being evergreen, ivies are ideal for providing cover in the autumn and winter months. Here, mixed ivies trail over a wall to meet autumn-flowering sedums and ferns.

AFTERCARE

Ivies appear to make little progress in their first year; they need this initial period for the establishment of roots below ground level. In their second year, however, the growth rate is much more obvious, and in later years it should be considerable.

Once well established, the growth rate of an ivy is considerable. With a little care it will be problem free, and will spread successfully like this *Hedera pastuchovii*.

Climbers Many gardeners seek fast-growing ivies, perhaps to cover an unsightly structure quickly, and enquire about growth rates. There are, however, no fixed rates of growth. Progress depends not only on the species and variety planted, but also on whether the ivy is planted in a cold or sheltered spot, on the soil quality, and on aftercare.

Water is the first need of newly-planted ivies. If you keep the soil around the plant from drying out, you will be guaranteed success.

Whether you are in a hurry for leaf cover or not, it is a mistake to force the young plants with excessive feeding. Inorganic fertilizer, if it is applied before the plants are established enough to use the nutrients, has the reverse effect and can harm them.

In their first year, make sure that the newly-planted ivies do not dry out. A well-maintained mulch is a great help in retaining moisture, but it must be renewed from time to time, as some of the mulch will be scratched away by birds or taken into the soil by earthworms.

Some ivies seem to have difficulty in climbing certain surfaces. The cause of this may be that the surface is too smooth, because ivies prefer a rough texture to enable them to cling well. Another cause of failure to climb is that new brick walls often expel salts for the first few years, and this does not suit ivies. An old trick was to wash new walls with liquid manure. This may work, not for any nutritional value in the manure, but because its acid nature could possibly neutralize the salts. If you have a problem with new walls, you might prefer to wash the surface down with water and a little detergent.

Difficulty in clinging, however, is usually due to the action of wind. Even a position that appears to be sheltered can be a problem, because once the breeze has loosened the stems, it will not allow the tips to grip again.

It is best to be patient. Tuck in the waving stems behind those that have gripped the wall, or trim them off altogether and allow the ivy to concentrate its efforts on the stems that are clinging. An alternative is to give the ivies some help. This will have to be done in any case with the *colchica* varieties.

A good method is to fix metal eyes at the base and at the top of the wall or fence, say 30cm (1ft) apart. Wire can then be secured vertically between the eyes. Plastic-covered wire, usually a green colour to allow it to blend in with foliage, is available for this purpose and is easy to cut and twist on to the eyes.

The stems of the ivies can be tied to the wires as they grow. Use soft filis twine for tying; do not use polypropylene twine or plastic-coated wire ties. Even if you promise

ABOVE Ivies can be trained to grow up around a door, trimmed when necessary, to make an elegant framework of foliage.

LEFT A healthy *Hedera colchica* 'Dentata Variegata' integrated into a walled garden.

yourself to replace these later, you will not be able to find them all and in due time the wire will sever the growing stems.

In their second year and onwards, climbing ivies may be fed during the growing season with a balanced fertilizer, such as Growmore, worked into the surface.

Eventually, ivies on walls and fences may need a trim. As the ivy progresses, the leaves on the lower stems sometimes become aged and perhaps brown. These should be stripped off completely, just leaving bare stems. At the same time, trim away the tips of the leading shoots at the top. The ivy will respond by growing new fresh leaves from top to bottom. Trimming may be done at any time of year.

When your ivy reaches the top of the wall you may see signs of its wish to flower and seed. If you want

ABOVE Allow ivies used as ground cover to settle down for a year or so before using a fertilizer.

BELOW *Hedera helix* 'Ester' used as ground cover, a most effective way of using ivies.

to keep it juvenile, you must trim off the arborescent growth as it appears. Most gardeners, however, enjoy the sight of flowers and berries.

Ground cover In the first year, water is an essential need. When established, ivies are very drought tolerant, and even in very dry years watering should not be needed as long as you maintain a mulch.

Allow ground-cover ivies to become established before attempting to encourage them with inorganic fertilizer. Weeds should be removed by hand to reduce competition, and the mulch maintained.

In the second year, and each following spring, scatter Growmore or a similar granular, balanced fertilizer between the plants to see them through the year.

Eventually, ground-cover ivies will need a trim. This can be done with shears, just as you would clip a hedge. In the USA, where ivies are very commonly grown as ground cover, grass mowers are set at their highest limit and run over the ivies. However, such drastic treatment should not normally be required. If the ivies are not kept low to the ground by trimming, however, the original stems will become quite thick after a number of years. The answer is to cut the centre of such plants right away, leaving younger stems to rejuvenate the beds.

Containers Much more watering is needed for ivies in pots, troughs and baskets than for plants in other situations, and this in return depletes the nutrient content of the compost. Consequently, ivies in pots need to be fed with inorganic fertilizer even in the first year. Liquid feeding is perhaps best, and a foliar feed with a spray is helpful. A slow-release fertilizer is almost as good.

BELOW Trim ground cover ivies over with shears to keep them neat and low.

BOTTOM Ensure that ivies in containers are fed and watered regularly.

21

PROPAGATION

As long as you follow one or two basic rules, you do not need green fingers to propagate ivies. You can easily increase your stocks either from cuttings or by layering stems. It is a good idea to have spare plants for replacement purposes in case of losses. And when a friend admires a particular ivy, how pleasant it is to be able to say, 'I have a young plant I can let you have.'

LEFT Choose an ivy trail with roots growing opposite the leaf nodes for layering.

RIGHT Take cuttings which have three leaves each. Remove the lower leaf, and push three to five cuttings into a pot of compost up to the second leaf node.

Plants from cuttings Before you take your cuttings you must gather together all the things you need: a sharp knife or garden scissors; hormone rooting powder; compost; a pot; a polythene bag of a size to go over the pot and cuttings; an elastic band, and a plant label. You can dispense with the polythene bag if you have a propagator.

The compost may be any proprietary soilless mixture; one containing sand is ideal. If you want to mix your own, use a formula of two parts peat, one part chopped bark and one part grit or coarse sand.

The size of pot depends on how many cuttings you want to take. It is best to keep to pots no larger than 9cm (3½in) and use more if you need them. Fill the pots with the compost, water well and stand them to drain.

Take your cuttings from new growth. Although July is the very best time, cuttings may be taken any time from May until October. Cut a healthy and good-looking trail with well-spaced leaves. If tiny shoots are showing at the leaf joints, so much the better.

Now you can cut the trail into cuttings. Each cutting should have three leaves. The tip of the trail should be discarded.

Remove the lower leaf and dip the stem into the hormone rooting powder, tapping off the surplus. Push the stem of the cutting into the compost up to the second leaf joint or node. With large-leaved ivies, you should insert three cuttings in a 9cm (3½in) pot. With medium-sized leaves, insert five cuttings per pot, spacing them evenly, and with small-leaved sorts you may be able to fit in up to eight cuttings.

The aim is to cover the compost completely with the leaves of the cuttings. When you are satisfied, water the cuttings well.

allowed into the bag. After a few days the bag can be removed.

If, however, the cutting comes away and has no roots, put it back, reseal the bag and try again in a couple of weeks.

Layering This is the simplest way of propagating an ivy and needs no special equipment, glasshouse or propagator.

In the case of layering, the roots of the potential new plant are produced while it is still attached to and fed by its parent.

You may layer directly into the soil surrounding the parent plant and later dig out the new plant, complete with a small root ball. However, it is better to root the stem into pots of special compost, which are set in the soil. These can then be lifted when the time comes without disturbing the young plant at all.

If you adopt this latter method, you will require some 8cm (3in) pots. These should be filled with damp compost as described under Cuttings. You will also need some pieces of galvanized wire, each about 10cm (4in) long, bent into pegs.

Select a nice long trail on the ivy that you want to increase. Choose one with tiny roots just showing opposite the nodes or leaf joints. Mark where these fall with sticks.

Gently move the trail to one side and trowel out holes the size of the pots at the points marked by the sticks. Next, bury the pots with their rims level with the soil surface.

Replace the ivy trail, and peg the stem into the compost just next to each marked leaf joint. That is all you need do for a month or more. Do not be in a hurry to sever a young plant from its parent; wait until the roots are really well established, then make a clean cut when the pot and new ivy can be lifted away.

If you have a propagator, you need do no more than place the pot in it. If not, cover the cuttings with the polythene bag and secure it around the pot with the elastic band.

Cuttings need humidity to reduce the loss of moisture, gentle warmth in the compost to encourage rooting, and light for photosynthesis. You should be able to find a place that will meet these requirements either on a window-sill in your home or in the glasshouse or conservatory, but shade cuttings from direct sun, especially through glass.

Leave well alone for about three weeks, then lift the bag and gently tug a cutting. If there is resistance, this means that the roots have formed and a little air may now be

PESTS AND DISEASES

Ivies outdoors are largely free from pests and diseases. The problems that do come their way are easily solved. Ivies indoors or under glass are quite a different matter, and here it is best to try to avoid the conditions that encourage troublesome pests.

PESTS

Red spider mite Also known as the two-spotted mite, *Tetranychus urticae* thrives in warm, dry conditions. Ivies planted outdoors on hot south-facing walls will sometimes, in warm summers, play host to this unwelcome pest. Ivies that are indoors and have been allowed to dry out will also attract it. Severe infestations can be fatal to a plant.

The mite is almost impossible to see. What you will observe is the damage that it causes to the leaves by sucking the sap. A pale-yellow stipple on the underside of leaves is the tell-tale sign.

Out of doors, the answer is to spray well, with an insecticide that has systemic activity such as 'Sybol' that controls red spider mite. Spray until the liquid runs off the leaves freely; you will find that this is also an effective cure for pot-grown ivies.

For ivies grown under glass, biological control of red spider mite is available in the form of the predator *Phytoseiulus perimilis*. However, the ordinary gardener does not usually have a sufficient infestation to keep the predator population going, and they will die out.

Scale Soft scale, *Cocus hesperidum*, and other scale insects sometimes infest climbing ivies and houseplant ivies. This is not a serious pest, and a small infestation can be removed quite easily by scraping the insects off the backs of the leaves. If they survive this treatment, they will succumb easily to spraying with a systemically active insecticide such as 'Sybol'.

Aphids Blackfly and greenfly will gather on the tips of young ivies, particularly in spring. Again, this is not a serious or long-lived problem,

ABOVE RIGHT Vine weevil grubs, enlarged.

LEFT This *Hedera helix* 'Fantasia' is thriving in a conservatory, but ivies grown indoors or under glass can be prone to pests.

and minor infestations can be rubbed off the tips with a paint-brush. Spraying with a systemically active insecticide such as 'Rapid' will deal with a stronger attack. For glasshouses, biological control is available in the form of a parasitic wasp, *Encarsia formosa*, but it is not really suitable for small-scale growers.

Vine weevil The grub stage of this weevil, *Otiorhynchus sulcatus*, has become a severe pest of pot-grown plants in recent years, since the ban on aldrin. The vine weevil will not make ivy its first choice in the garden, but when an adult lays her eggs in a pot of ivy, the grubs that emerge have little choice but to eat the roots. The first sign of trouble is a wilted ivy, by which time it is usually too late for a successful rescue.

Chemical treatments are not available to gardeners. Biological control can be obtained by using a parasitic nematode called *Heterorhabitis*, which is marketed under the name 'Nemasys'. Again, however, this biological method is not really suitable for small numbers of pot plants.

The easiest, cheapest and safest method of control is to repot your ivies annually, or, better still, twice a year. Weevil grub damage will be obvious from the lack of root system, and the pale cream grubs, less than 1cm (⅓in) long, can easily be seen against the dark compost and removed. Repot in August and, if you can, do this again in February.

DISEASES

Ivy leaf spot Few problems of disease affect ivies, but a fungal disease that sometimes appears in wet summers is ivy leaf spot, *Colletotrichum trichellum*. Brown spots about 1cm (⅜in) across make the leaves look unsightly. In the early stages, cutting off the spotted leaves, or just the affected parts on the large-leaved *colchica* varieties, will prevent the spread of the trouble. A fungicide spray such as 'Nimrod'-T will arrest ivy leaf spot should it get beyond the 'cutting-out' stage.

Much less often seen is a similar problem, the difference here being that the spots are larger and black. This can be either bacterial leaf spot, *Xanthomonas hederae*, or black leaf spot, *Phyllosticta hedericola*, a fungus. The early stages can be cured in the same way as for ivy leaf spot. There is no spray for use against the bacterial leaf spot, but the black leaf spot can be controlled with 'Nimrod'-T.

Fungal problems Botrytis is only rarely a problem, though it occasionally occurs during the propagation of cuttings, when temperatures are too low for quick rooting. Either increased warmth or spraying with fungicide such as Benlate+ 'Activex' 2 will soon correct this.

IVIES AS HOUSEPLANTS

Ivy is in the top ten list of houseplants, and thousands of small young plants are sold each year by supermarkets and large high street stores. Growers choose colourful and distinct sorts that lend themselves to pots because of their bushy nature. These are called 'self-branching' ivies because they are short jointed and throw branches readily, compared with the climbing varieties, which have their leaves well spaced on a few long leaders or vines.

Ivies complement all houseplants and can be grown in any number of settings. Here they flank a graceful window-box display of cyclamen and *Chamaedara*, helping to soften the outlines of the container and providing a pleasing contrast in leaf shape.

There are exceptions, such as the green and variegated *canariensis*, which make excellent indoor plants, mainly for tall displays.

The quality of plants offered by the large multiple stores is of the very highest. Indeed, the plants look so lush and bright that one often hears the question 'Are they real?'

This quality is obtained by propagating and growing the plants in a closely-controlled environment at warm temperatures. It follows that you will have either to provide a similar habitat at home or gradually harden the plants off, acclimatizing them to more everyday conditions.

The difficulties encountered in this initial period are the usual reason for failure with houseplant ivies. Another common cause of losses is when the pots are allowed to dry out in summer or, conversely, given too much water in winter.

How to succeed Once home, put your newly-purchased ivy in a light place, but away from direct sunlight, especially if it is shining through glass. If the compost seems dry, water it from the top, with the pot standing in a deep saucer. After 30 minutes, any surplus water in the saucer should be tipped away.

Leave the plant for a week or so, keeping the compost damp, until it has made a little growth to prove that it has settled into its new environment.

Now it is time to think about a more permanent life for your plant. Most supermarket ivies are grown in peat-based compost in 8cm (3in) pots. These composts dry out quickly and have little body to sustain the amount of growth an ivy can make, and the pots will soon be outgrown.

Repot into 12cm (5in) or 15cm (6in) pots, using a soil-based com-

TOP Ivies lend them-
selves to imaginative
indoor use, as with this
small stone sculpture.

ABOVE A hanging
basket is ideal for
ivies such as *Hedera
helix* 'Pittsburgh'.

post; John Innes No. 3 is ideal. If you repot an ivy in winter, make sure that the compost is warm and do not take it directly from a frozen bag.

Feeding and watering From early April until October feed with half-strength liquid fertilizer every time you water. This may seem excessive, especially during warm periods, when you may need to water once or twice a week. The nutrients in com-

post are soon used up, however, and the mass of foliage that an ivy will make, particularly in relation to the small size of its roots, dictates this constant need.

Give a thorough wetting, using a deep saucer and making sure that the plant takes all it needs; wait until liquid remains in the saucer. After half an hour, tip away the surplus. Do this as often as required, but do not waterlog the plant.

From November until March, keep the compost as dry as you dare. Do not feed the plant, and water the compost only sparingly, as little as once every four to six weeks. As a supplement, you can spray the foliage; this is particularly important in centrally-heated rooms, but not so vital if your ivies are growing in a bathroom, kitchen or conservatory.

Americans are very successful with indoor ivies because they keep, as a matter of course, a small spray next to their plants, and use it every time they pass by.

General points Most ivies that fail indoors do so due to a combination of too much water and too little light. A dark corner is no place for a plant, even if it is a shade lover; remember that without light the ivy cannot grow. When it is not growing, an ivy needs no water. If you water in these circumstances, you are literally drowning the plant by driving the oxygen from its roots.

Keeping ivy roots damp in summer and dry in winter is the key to success, but learning how to assess the amount of water that is needed can prove difficult. The best method is to get used to the weight of the plant. Water one plant and not another, then feel the difference in weight; you will soon be able to judge, just by lifting a pot, whether the plant is in need of water.

27

SIXTY OF THE BEST

Some of the ivies here are old varieties, dating back to the 1800s; others are recent and unusual cultivars. Many are readily available at garden centres, where the most popular varieties are usually stocked. The others are available from leading general nurseries and from specialist ivy nurseries. The annual guide *The Plant Finder*, published by the Hardy Plant Society, will help you to locate these.

Hedera *helix*
'Midas Touch'

The glossy leaves of *Hedera canariensis* 'Algerian'

Hedera azorica
'Typica'

The species form of *azorica*, this is an ivy with a large matt leaf of a distinctive shape that is unlike any other. It has five to seven lobes; these are covered with soft pale hair, which gives the leaves a light-green look. This fast-growing vining ivy is suitable as a climber and very hardy.

'Variegata'

A beautifully variegated vining ivy, this has cream-yellow leaves that are splashed, spotted, striped and stippled with green. Like the green form, it has five or seven lobes, but it is not quite so vigorous in growth. At first glance, this ivy looks as if it might be tender, but it is not, and will come through hard winters without problems.

Hedera canariensis
'Algerian'

The vigorous and fast-growing green ivy from North Africa has large, glossy unlobed leaves on wine-red stems. A vining ivy, this climbs well but is useful for all purposes, since it covers ground at a good pace. Its leaves can be damaged in hard winters, but new ones appear in spring. This species tolerates drought conditions well. You may find this ivy under the names 'Montgomery' or 'Ravensholst', but botanists would prefer to call it *algeriensis*.

'Gloire de Marengo'

A variegated Algerian cultivar, this has large unlobed cream leaves with central grey-green splashes set on wine-red stems. It is well known as a pot plant, but is best in the garden, where it needs plenty of space, as it is very robust and fast to grow. This is a vining ivy, good for climbing and for ground cover. It is sometimes named *canariensis* 'Variegata'.

'Margina Maculata'

Another variegated Algerian, this has pale lemon-cream leaves splashed and spotted with green. The overall effect is very much lighter than 'Gloire de Marengo'. The large area of cream can make the leaves look rather unsightly when they have suffered winter damage, but this cultivar is nevertheless well worth risking, since it is at its best a very handsome and spectacular vining ivy.

Hedera colchica
'Dentata'
The unlobed, matt leaves of the green Persian ivy are often up to 22 cm (9 in) long, so it is not surprising to find that it is sometimes called 'Elephant Ears'. This very hardy, vining ivy is a superb climber, but requires some help. Perhaps it is even better used as ground cover, tumbling over a low wall or from the edge of a pool.

'Dentata Variegata'
A variegated Persian ivy, this has creamy-yellow large unlobed leaves, with central splashes of light green. It is a vining ivy, and will give dense cover either to a wall or on the ground, but it will need help if grown as a climber. This is among the most spectacular of ivies, never losing its variegation; it grows well, and is extremely hardy.

'Sulphur Heart'
Another colourful Persian ivy, its variegation is the reverse of 'Dentata Variegata', the large, unlobed green leaves having a central splash of pale yellow. Often wrongly called 'Paddy's Pride', this is a vining ivy and is wonderful either as a climber, in which case it needs help, or as ground cover.

H. ca. 'Gloire de Marengo'

H. ca. 'Margina Maculata'

Hedera colchica 'Sulphur Heart'

31

Hedera helix
'Adam'
This is a bushy, white-cream varie-gated ivy. The edges of its small three-lobed leaves turn pink outside in winter. It is a self-branching ivy and, being bushy, it is very suitable for trailing purposes. 'Adam' never seems to revert to green, and it makes a good houseplant.

'Angularis Aurea'
One of the best aureus forms, this has glossy medium-sized leaves. In spring, the leaves are yellow, and these are followed by mottled yellow-green leaves in summer, and entirely green leaves in autumn. Being a vining ivy, it is a climber, and one that clings very well on its own without help. It grows reason-ably quickly in any aspect, but shows more colour in good light, where there is sun during part of the day. When you buy young plants they will be green, sometimes with just a hint of the aureus to follow. It can take two years or more for the plant to show its potential.

'Anne Marie'
This beautiful ivy, sometimes known as 'Harald', has a bright-cream variegation that is enhanced by outside conditions. It is self-branching, with long trails, which makes it perfect if you are looking for a plant that will tumble from containers, window-boxes and hang-ing baskets. It will climb, too, if given the chance. The ample leaves have five indistinct lobes on green stems.

'Atropurpurea'
The leaves of this green vining ivy turn a deep purple with the onset of cold weather in autumn. This is not the darkest of the 'purple' ivies – 'Glymii' is darker – but it has an interesting leaf shape and clings and climbs very well. The arrow-shaped leaves of the young plant are repla-ced by larger ones, with five distinct lobes, as the plant matures.

'Bowles Ox Heart'
This very bold green ivy has become naturalized in certain parts of Bri-tain. It deserves a place in this list

Hedera helix 'Adam'

H.h. 'Angularis Aurea'

32

H.h. 'Buttercup' has attractive yellow leaves

because of its outstanding vigour and hardiness. E. A. Bowles called it the 'Ox' or 'Bullock's Heart', and it can still be found in his garden. In Scotland, the same plant has been named 'Argyle Street', but so long after Bowles' description as to make this later name invalid. The leaves look, at first glance, like those of the Algerian ivy, but without the gloss. This vining ivy is suitable for fast vertical or horizontal cover.

'Brokamp'
This is a very bushy green self-branching ivy, with willow-like medium-sized leaves. A single specimen makes a nice-looking pot plant, but this cultivar is also one of the best ivies for ground cover. As it matures, the unlobed leaves broaden, becoming spear-shaped. It is one of the few ivies to remain bright green in winter, when most ivies bronze to some degree.

'Buttercup'
Planted where it receives direct sun, this vining ivy will reward you with a bright display of buttercup-yellow leaves. These are small and retain their colour all the year through. Although this ivy is suitable only for climbing, it does not always cling readily, and if the planting position does not suit it, it can be very slow to grow to any size. This is one ivy that will benefit from some humus around its roots to give it a good start. It is often confused with 'Angularis Aurea' or 'Succinata', so pay particular attention to the colour illustration here before you buy to make sure you're choosing the correct cultivar.

'Caenwoodiana Aurea'
The green bird's foot ivy, called 'Pedata' and described below, is a very popular climbing ivy. This is the aureus form of it. It is a vining ivy, and suitable only for climbing, but its nature of showing patchy yellow colour, especially in spring, makes this a very worthwhile cultivar. The medium-sized leaves are distinctly akin to the indentation a bird's foot leaves on wet sand.

33

'Ceridwen'
The name means fair and graceful, and is most appropriate for this golden form. Its pointed leaves are yellow, with bold brush strokes in two tones of green. Self-branching, with plenty of trails, this ivy is one of the best to select for pots, containers and hanging baskets. It is much more bushy than 'Goldchild', which it resembles in colour.

'Chester'
This self-branching ivy with long trails has lovely lemon-cream variegation on medium-sized, triangular-shaped leaves. It looks delicate, but is in fact hardy. A wonderful sight on a dark wall, 'Chester' is suitable for all purposes, because it will both trail and climb.

H.h. 'Chester'

'Conglomerata'
A very distinct dwarfed ivy, this has small, dark-green leaves that are leathery and crinkled, growing very closely on short woody stems. It only grows horizontally, will not spread too far, and will not climb, making it a true prostrate form, ideal for stone gardens and stone walls.

'Deltoidea'
This ivy has heart-shaped leaves, which is why it is called 'Sweetheart Ivy' in the USA. The medium-to-small leaves are very deep green and can turn bronze in winter. It is popular with flower arrangers, not only for its obvious uses for romantic celebrations, but because its stems are stiff and lend themselves to arrangement without difficulty. A reluctant climber, it is best used for ground cover.

'Direktor Badke'
Small, round mid-green leaves on a very bushy self-branching plant make this ivy perfect for patio gar-

H.h. 'Conglomerata'

dening, for hanging baskets and for all trailing purposes. It can also be an unusual and effective choice for small areas of ground cover.

'Dragon Claw'
A good-looking ivy with unusual leaves that are medium to large in size and deeply curled, this is a modestly self-branching cultivar with long trails. It climbs very well and also makes good ground cover, but it is rather too vigorous for containers.

'Duckfoot'
This self-branching ivy throws a mass of well-covered trails. It has tiny, mid-green leaves in the shape of a duck's foot, which makes it an interesting pot specimen, fascinating to children.

'Eva'
Here is a small-leaved variegated self-branching ivy that enjoys climbing. The three-lobed leaves are a strong shade of cream, splashed with two tones of green in their centre. 'Eva' is an all-purpose ivy of good temper and hardiness.

'Erecta'
One of the candelabra ivies, with stiff self-supporting stems covered with cupped leaves, this becomes a

H.h. 'Dragon Claw'

fine individual shrub up to 1.2m (4ft) high after a few years. 'Erecta' can make a quite unusual garden feature, especially if several are grown as a group.

'Filigran'
This is a rich-green, compact, self-branching ivy, with very crimped and curled leaves. It is perhaps at its best when grown as a pot specimen, but well worth trying for other purposes, since it always provokes comment on its unusual appearance.

H.h. 'Deltoidea'

H.h. 'Duckfoot'

'Fleur de lis'
This distinctive green cultivar is well named, as its leaf shape strongly resembles the French royal insignia. A somewhat self-branching ivy, with long trails, it climbs well and also covers ground.

'Fluffy Ruffles'
The name characterizes this cultivar, which does not look like an ivy at all. The light-green leaves are like frilled rosettes, so deeply are they waved and curled, making this an obvious choice for a pot specimen.

'Glacier'
A silver-grey ivy – hence the name – this is popular for several reasons: it retains its variegation out of doors; it is self-branching, so that it covers ground well, and it is a particularly hardy, variegated sort. It will also climb, if given the chance, but is at its best when simply allowed to trail.

H.h. 'Fluffy Ruffles'

H.h. 'Glacier'

'Glymii'

This is the darkest of the 'purple' ivies, the great difference between this cultivar and the other dark sorts lying in its glossy leaves. It is, of course, green in summer, when it is quite undistinguished. A vining ivy, which makes a good climber, its winter trails are much sought after by flower arrangers.

H.h. 'Goldchild'

'Goldchild'

This beautiful golden ivy was originally such a weak specimen that it was in danger of becoming extinct. However, a really robust clone was found, and 'Goldchild' has now been re-established as perhaps the best all-round golden ivy. First introduced as a pot ivy, it is now used for all outdoor purposes. Although self-branching, it climbs readily.

'Gold Dust'

There are several names for this speckled ivy: 'Luzii' is one, 'Masquerade' another, and 'Golden Pittsburgh' a third. All the names were originally valid, but the differences between these varieties have over the years become merged. The leaves are small to medium, with five lobes of mottled light grey green, overstippled with yellow. This is a self-branching ivy, suitable for all trailing purposes. 'California Gold' is similar, but has convoluted leaves.

H.h. 'Gold Dust' is a beautiful trailing ivy

'Golden Ingot'

A most attractive golden self-branching ivy with five round lobed leaves, this cultivar features a generously golden-yellow variegation, spotted and splashed with two tones of green. Its bushy habit and delicate colours make this a first-class specimen to grow as a houseplant or in a featured pot outside.

'Goldheart'

Everyone's favourite gold climber, this has dark-green leaves, small to medium in size, with a bright splash of yellow in the centre. It is ubiquitous, but do not let this put you off; its popularity should not lessen the value of this lovely ivy. It has been described as the best vining ivy ever introduced, and who could doubt this after seeing a good specimen on a sun-drenched wall in spring? 'Goldheart' is suitable only as a climber, and its red-pink stems cling very well without help. It will throw the occasional green stem, which should be pulled off as soon as it is seen.

H.h. 'Goldheart'

The golden-yellow variegation of *H.h.* 'Golden Ingot'

H.h. 'Green Ripple' is versatile and appealing

'Green Ripple'

This elegant and attractive ivy has rippling rich-green and distinctly forward-pointing leaves of medium size, with their five marked lobes and prominent pale veins which add to its beautiful, lush appearance. It is self-branching, but is capable of climbing very successfully. It is also extremely hardy and therefore recommended for all garden purposes, from ground cover to training up walls or trailing from tubs or urns.

'Helena'

This is a silver-variegated ivy with arrow-shaped leaves, distinguished by the slight curve to left or right of its long terminal lobe. A most attrative self-branching ivy, this is useful for trailing, especially if used in association with dark-coloured ivies or other darker plants.

'Hibernica Hamilton'

No list of recommended ivy cultivars would be complete without mention

39

The striking leaves of *H.h.* 'Hibernica Variegata'

of 'Hibernica', commonly known as the Irish ivy. 'Hamilton' is a selection from the standard form, this one having deep-bronze leaves during the winter months. 'Hibernica' is perhaps the vining ivy that is most widely used for ground cover, particularly in public places, not only in the UK but all over the world.

'Hibernica Variegata'
There has been some confusion over the years about this name. Here, it is applied to the yellow-variegated Irish ivy. The cream-white variegated form with which the name is confused should, according to modern nomenclature, be called 'Hibernica Latimaculata'. The yellow form is much more constant than the white cultivar, and makes a spectacular specimen. Some leaves will be wholly green; others wholly yellow, and more half and half. This cultivar has the large leaves of 'Hibernica' and is a vining ivy, suitable only for use as a climber.

H.h. 'Irish Lace'

40

'Irish Lace'

There is a very bushy green self-branching ivy, with finely-fingered leaves, that is incorrectly called 'Sagittifolia'; but that name belongs to an old vining ivy of the 1800s which has distinctly arrow-shaped leaves. A very similar ivy, but not so finely fingered, is said to have been selected in Germany by Herr Koniger in 1935; hence the name 'Koniger's Auslese'. All these ivies – and there are others – have in common striking leaves with five long tapering lobes, and the best of the lot is the one which is known as 'Irish Lace'. This is such an attractive cultivar that it is almost indispensable for using in hanging baskets throughout the year.

'Ivalace'

Ivies are ivies, but every once in a while a new cultivar tends to come along which manages to outshine all the rest with its sheer beauty. 'Ivalace' is such a one. The leaves are a rich, glossy bronze green, and have finely-crimped margins and narrow yellow veining, which gives the plant an intricate, lacy look. It holds its stems erect as a young plant, which makes it particularly suitable for growing in pots. This is a hardy ivy and therefore quite happy in the garden, where it makes an interesting choice for ground cover or an unlikely but effective and unusual climber for a low wall.

H.h. 'Ivalace'

H.h. 'Kolibri'

'Kolibri'
This is a speckled white-variegated ivy, and in fact 'variable' should be its middle name, for it is so variable that the resulting confusion has given rise to half a dozen different names. None of these variations is likely to be constant for long, but this should not deter you from planting 'Kolibri', since it is a most attractive sort and its variegation is all part of its charm. Used mainly for container work and for trailing, it can in fact climb, and looks particularly striking on an old tree trunk.

'Lalla Rookh'
The very striking medium-to-large leaves of this ivy have spiky lobes that fold and overlap, and feature prominent pale veins on a ground of rich green. The ivy is modestly self-branching, with long trails, and lends itself to all purposes where a strong

H.h. 'Little Diamond'

H.h. 'Manda's Crested'

H.h. 'Midas Touch', superb for container planting

ivy is wanted. It climbs and trails, but is too large for using in small pots and baskets.

'Little Diamond'

This is a useful variegated sort because it is not invasive. It is ideal for the front of a border, where it can be underplanted with spring bulbs. As the name implies, it has diamond-shaped leaves; these are small and are a grey green, with white on the edges. This is a self-branching ivy, and pleasant in containers, but not in any way a climber.

'Manda's Crested'

This used to be called 'Curly Locks', which describes its form well. It was the first of the now-numerous curly ivies, and remains the most vigorous. It looks very attractive in pots and containers. The edges of its large, pea-green leaves often show a delicate purple tint, and plants that are used outside as ground cover take on a slightly bronze look in winter. 'Manda's Crested' is modestly self-branching.

'Marginata Major'

One of the old climbing varieties, this has creamy-yellow variegation on the edge of small-to-medium, lobeless, almost diamond-shaped leaves. The grey-green centre splashes are cut with prominent cream veins. The vines cling very successfully and give good cover.

'Midas Touch'

The bright gold splashes on the leaves of this exciting form are heightened by the contrast with the deep rich-green background and pink-red stems. Its convoluted leaf shape and self-branching habit make this the most outstanding yellow-variegated ivy available for growing in pots and containers.

The distinctive leaves of *H.h.* 'Parsley Crested'

'Mrs Pollock'

A most unusual reluctantly-aureus form, this vining ivy dates from 1885 and, when used as a climber, its leaves hang in a most attractive manner like half-opened fans. In good sunlight, it can show a golden tint, but this can take a few years.

'Parsley Crested'

This is a bold, somewhat self-branching, green ivy with distinctive crimped edges to its round leaves, giving it a 'parsley' effect. It is often, but incorrectly, called 'Cristata'. It will climb and makes good ground cover, but the crimping on the leaves is much more pronounced when the plant is confined to a pot or container. A recent development from 'Parsley Crested', called 'Melanie', has a lovely mauve edge to its leaves, but this variety is not yet widely available.

'Pedata'

This unmistakable vining ivy has leaves that are divided like the toes of a bird's foot. Its dull green colour and white veins gave rise to the alternative name 'Grey Arrow'.

H.h. 'Poetica'

Suitable only for climbing, it has narrow leaves that are well spaced on long stems, making this an ideal ivy for a good-looking wall, since the latter will not be blanked out completely.

'Poetica'

Most ivies in this list are here because of their leaves, but 'Poetica' owes its place to the berries of the adult form, for while all other ivies produce black fruits, 'Poetica' produces pale orange berries. If you want to grow it as a climber, try to purchase seedlings that are guaran-

H.h. 'Sagittifolia Variegata' makes good ground cover

H.h. 'Succinata'

teed to have been grown from orange berries. In other respects the plant is identical to 'Hibernica', and is perhaps best grown as a tree ivy, so that the berries can be seen even on a tiny plant.

'Professor Friedrich Tobler'
In this unmistakable variation the leaves of the three main lobes are almost completely divided. The leaves are mid-green in colour, and the plant is self-branching, with long trails, which makes it a very suitable companion to flowering plants in a hanging basket.

'Sagittifolia Variegata'
This very attractive, self-branching ivy, with small-fingered leaves, has cream-white variation. It is a most useful, bushy plant for pots and containers, where it trails well and retains its bright colour. It is quite hardy, so it is suitable for winter hanging baskets, and it also makes beautiful ground cover under conifers and in similar dark areas.

'Spetchley'
This is the variety with the smallest leaves, much smaller than your fingernail, and is very useful for rock crevices or between paving stones. It looks particularly pretty at the very edge of a border under-planted with snowdrops, and is a true miniature – a real gem.

'Succinata'
One of the old varieties, this dates from the 1800s, when it was descri-bed as 'the amber-leafed ivy'. In winter, the leaves are a rich bronze green, almost wine coloured. In spring, the new growth explodes into a golden amber colour. It is strongly vining and an excellent climber.

45

'Sulphurea'
The name of this very old ivy at once gives an accurate impression of the appearance of this strong and hardy climber. The grey-green and sulphury-yellow leaves pucker and curl to hide their lobes. This is a bold and vigorous form, and is well suited for ground cover.

'Tess'
Bold leaves with a mosaic of gold between light-yellow veins is the promise of this strong climbing ivy. When you will be rewarded with this tessellar blush of gold is a matter of luck and whether it is in a sunny situation. Even without the gold, you will have a strong climbing ivy with attractive, prominently-veined green leaves.

H.h. 'Tess', a strong climber

'Tricolor'
This small-leaved ivy's claim to fame lies in its pink edge, which strengthens in colour with the onset of winter weather. Its leaves are rather sparsely spaced on wiry vines, so this variety is perhaps best intertwined with another lightly-covering green form, such as 'Pedata'.

Hedera nepalensis
'Typica'
Obviously from Nepal, this species form is well worth growing for the classical effect of its drooping, serrated leaves, which are held on reddish stems. It is a vining ivy, suitable only as a climber.

Hedera pastuchovii
'Typica'
The Russian ivy's long, unlobed

The graceful *Hedera nepalensis* 'Typica'

leaves have a blue-green hue and hang to make an attractive feature. It is a vining ivy, quite strong in growth, and hardy. It is suitable for wall covering, as it will cling well without help.

Hedera rhombea 'Variegata'

The variegated Japanese ivy has most delicate spoon-shaped leaves of blue green, with a thin white edge. It is rather slow growing and slightly wiry, so you should set it to climb small areas rather than vast walls. It is pretty and elegant, and makes an unusual pot ivy, in which case it can be kept trimmed to encourage it to become bushy.

Hedera pastuchovii 'Typica'

47

INDEX AND ACKNOWLEDGEMENTS

Page numbers in **bold type** indicate illustrations

Picture credits

Gillian Beckett: 7, 18, 44(t,cr), 45(t). The Garden Picture Library: 27 (tl).
John Glover: 12(t), 28-29, 34(b), 36(t), 40(br), 42(tl,br), 43, 45(cl), 46.
Derek Gould: 8, 17(tr), 31(br), 38(tr), 47(br).
Marshall Cavendish Library: 27(cl), 36(br).
S. & O. Matthews: 4-5.
Tania Midgley: 10(b).
Harry Smith Horticultural Collection: 1, 6, 10(cr), 12(br), 13(t), 16(tr,bl), 17(b), 19(tr,bl), 20(t,br), 21, 22, 27(h), 32(bl), 33.
Michael Warren: 13(b), 14, 15, 24, 25, 26, 31(tr), 35(br), 37(tl), 39.
Ronald Whitehouse: 30, 31(bl), 32(br), 34(t), 35(tr,bl), 37(b), 38(b), 40(t), 41, 42(bl), 47(t).